# THE LATE PARADE

*Adam Fitzgerald*

LIVERIGHT PUBLISHING CORPORATION
A DIVISION OF W. W. NORTON & COMPANY
NEW YORK LONDON

# THE LATE PARADE

*Poems*

"For the Marriage of Faustus and Helen" from *White Buildings* by Hart
Crane. Copyright © 1926 by Boni & Liveright, Inc. Copyright renewed
1954 by Liveright Publishing Corporation. Used by permission of Liveright
Publishing Corporation.

For information about permission to reproduce selections from this book,
write to Permissions, Liveright Publishing Corporation,
a division of W. W. Norton & Company, Inc.,
500 Fifth Avenue, New York, NY 10110

For information about special discounts for bulk purchases,
please contact W. W. Norton Special Sales
at specialsales@wwnorton.com or 800-233-4830

Manufacturing by Courier Westford
Book design by Lovedog Studio
Production manager: Anna Oler

Library of Congress Cataloging-in-Publication Data

Fitzgerald, Adam.
[Poems. Selections]
The late parade : poems / Adam Fitzgerald. — First edition.
    pages cm
Includes bibliographical references.
Poems.
ISBN 978-0-87140-674-3 (hardcover)
I. Title.
PS3606.I873L38 2013
811'.6—dc23
                                    2013000242

Liveright Publishing Corporation
500 Fifth Avenue, New York, N.Y. 10110
www.wwnorton.com

W. W. Norton & Company Ltd.
Castle House, 75/76 Wells Street, London W1T 3QT

    2 3 4 5 6 7 8 9 0

*for my parents*

&

*in memory of Christopher Catanese*
7.6.1983–7.6.2004

# Contents

*Grateful acknowledgments* are made to the editors of the magazines in which versions of these poems first appeared: *A Public Space, Agricultural Reader, The Battersea Review, BOMB, Boston Review, The Brooklyn Rail, Conjunctions, EOAGH: A Journal of the Arts, Fence, Jacket2, La Fovea, OmniVerse, OnAndOnScreen, Mead, The Miami Rail, Phoenix in the Jacuzzi Journal, Post Road, Ragazine, Southampton Literary Review, Statement of Record, Stonecutter, THEthe Poetry Blog, Washington Square Review.*

*There is the world dimensional for*
*those untwisted by the love of things*
*irreconcilable . . .*
                        —HART CRANE

CATHEDRAL

To write about one thing, you must first write about another.
To speak of the death of King Charles V,
you must first speak of the Hồ Chí Minh Dynasty.
To understand the rotund ministries of, say, moonlight,
you must first be blind, and understand fencing.

As for me, I understand discomfort. It falls
in the pinched, early blue bowl light of dawn.
I speak often and only erringly about football,
racket clubs, and the general way of the world.
You go out for coffee. You come back another person.

# STRANGE CINEMA

My ode to failure begins like a girl who awakens in a dream
and realizes the surface of her sleep over ungroomed clouds,
suspended in a vague pleasure of doubt. It continues on then
like a train departing from its track, sluicing invisible foam

and realizes the surface of . . . Her sleep over ungroomed clouds
troubled me. She failed too, the pungent musk of her hair
like a train departing from its track, sluicing invisible foam.
I don't care about any of this. I miss the person inside who

troubled me (she failed too). The pungent musk of her hair
is all that matters in the lobby where I slept, vacantly foraging.
I don't care about any of this. I miss the person inside who
hears nothing but the tracing of loss, some minor addenda.

Is all that matters in the lobby where I slept, vacantly foraging,
your shadow? Like cut pink fruit? A sudden shaft of sun?
Hear nothing but the tracing of loss, some minor addenda.
Or hear something, if you want, casually, a crevice in a name.

Your shadow like a cut of pink fruit, a sudden shaft of sun.
But that was before, when we could share our fumbled sex,
hearing something we wanted, casually, a crevice in a name,
in a room of lost boots, where the plum wallpaper was kind.

But that was before, when we could share our fumbled sex.
My ode to failure begins like a girl who awakens in a dream,
in a room of lost boots, where the plum wallpaper was kind.
Suspended in a vague pleasure of doubt, it continues on then.

# CARAVAGGIO IN NAPLES

*1*

It was a shock. A shock for everyone. Not exactly a killing
to be had, but from a zoneless dust, a millioned doodads
of pinkish/beige crumbcakes built in stuccoed stone, you

could almost taste the ageless warrens; baronial hodgepodge
shroomed on hill-jammed streets; the bay's smoky pines
wrestling for the stiff swim trunks of ancient summertime.

Slowly, you tongued the hardscrabble blood over two teeth
the showy city would soon obliviate as it dumbly dropped
postcard thoroughfares with a kind of lethal goldfish charm.

For all the overfurnished lye, the mildewed fringe, and shit,
you really had to hand it to the forgotten country. Awake,
eyeing fatty-handled souvenirs, tacky ormolu, lemon sorbets,

sometimes you were still asleep. Tumbling angelic bellies
broke through thrusted rainy domes, fixtures, holy tracts
about sanctions writ for viceroys, sexless men disquieted.

2

Thereafter, you licked the patent smudge off storied songs
   overheard inside stone-braided squares, linking arms
with hillbilly fairies, myopic at once for a new simplicity.

Scratching my crotch, I smiled at those parasitic stars.
   There they were in their big imperiality. Meanwhile,
wobbly-chinned truckers screwed their necks with no

what or why as babies dangled from a scooter's hump—
   the tart sky like another bum musing with his finger
how this year's been so noxiously accommodating here

in the city of the telescope, beginnings and endings
   of crass working credits, profiteering anarchic nitwits
and capers with a murky back agog in today's white-

trafficked chunks. Moreno gave a push. Ciro shaped
   afternoon scales neatly beside seatop-sleeping cranes.
Dancers' hips had movements tipsy as a mountaintop.

# 3

I was really tired, moody like a mongrel, fed up with facing
    home, frustrated by one foul thought that struck the pole of
    my forehead for anyone to read. Funnily, the sirroccoless city

mocked me with raging calm, new winds temperate as never,
    bantering like bathing huts as somewhere tawny shorts
meant nincompoops arranging boners like Social Democrats.

I've seen Ribera's beards, true. I've brushed shoulders with
    investigative journalists and their priest-strangled cuisine.
The shantytowns of parallel desire misfire, and trickle off.

I didn't fashion a swim yet daintily water swam before me
    in towel-drenched breezes where I could see the horizon
yawn Medusian concrete highways, enwebbing gaping cliffs

as if a few centuries of grids, ditch-spun lots, were nothing
    but Father Time snoring his sprawling, postmortem nap.
I guess I was every good consumer, except I wanted more.

4

To dribble past Volpi players, see hairy under-construction
   sites, pluck equipment then steal another innocuous pic
quite illicitly, lying down to wrap myself in a large T-shirt

big enough for the rest of the Sunday-tickled world. Gennaro
   had black-bluish hair, sparrow-eyed under ribboned knots.
Arcangelo arrested sex with paint in the shadow of a tricyclist.

Supper arrived with its geometric futilities, a nice smattering
   of Lao Tzu with chic design: great countries vs. small ones;
talk of fine designers who pinned their urchins with umlauts.

In five o'clock cocktail shadows, I saw perfumed cypresses
   and dozen-kilo engines slink around fabric-work, the night
I wondered why you left me lusting on the fence, stool-eyed,

all while a bra seemed to fall from heaven. Promiscuous
   friends rushed in from gold-hushed cloisterers in drag.
All these things at once, you said in that fumbling phrase.

5

One cannot be sincere and seem so too. I heard silk crunch under
  woolly light I found and fondled alone. So when you offered
your anonymity in shade, it was like a raincheck fulfilled, a visa

for corded countries made up beside that fountain over there.
  Tugs at moneylaundering we called our high-fashioned love.
Combing dirt from your plain clothes, I counted the dark stoops

where cabs tunneled by, your ear-chin-lip-nose-tongue piercings:
  what your face had to hold out to the world—figuring it no
 less profound than the Virgin's blue marquee, which was quite so.

I'm going to pen a letter now about the bourgie virtues, how to get
  lost, my own favored way. What else to unite these pebbles on
the jetset scape of a wet dream? Sober, in the new year, if the big

fruit tax lessens, as my colleagues warn with always-already
  unctions at the shortage, I'll hand you this cold dish I plucked
from a piece of earth, a herb, a thing to decorate my hearse.

# THE BRIDE

You could read to me about sesame clouds
and linen's appearance on sprawling walks.
Pouring your stiff, bright eyes in the avenue
would be one way, on the phone drawing
pink-splattered mist around tough eggshells,
another. You could heat rice and recite *Faust*,
batter an eyelash at the fringe resembling turf.

You could induce a brain rhythm set far back,
having a vague peripheral hint of horticulture:
a cornice of flower water sandwiching the air.
You could pull some covers over the ocean-bed,
deigning to peek at my crook cap and lip. You
could sit, a woman in a peach atrium, computer
on her lap, beckoning with the back of her head.

# THE RELAY STATION

We sleep in private homes now, forgetting
the laundry or whoever's name. Snow

comes and blankets, nothing about the outdoors
being lonely except it's the outdoors. The

same ones are opened. Piles of ghosted
marginalia end up at the end, where they

belong. A cord or two's tangled. Songs drift.
Soon, even sooner than that, what's tucked

inside isn't dark in the sense of darkness,
but resting like the-uncle-we-loved's hat.

Wide tracks of things we've thought about
cool into a frieze, waiting to be tracked

down one day until a loaned key is minted.
I or someone hums. Tissues are collected.

Dust settles. Our trust is newly renovated
like faucets, since fate's set that way, and today—

never happening—feels no more an impostor
than the rest of us, something not to be looked

on as anything but what fell between a casualty
of sorts. Woods or wares, as it were. News comes.

Furniture plays furniture. If what we exchange
rumbles in too much quiet, then it means this for you:

afternoon grievances or friends to be arranged.
Tea-steam purring from the kettle almost.

# THE MAP

I was shipwrecked on an island of clouds.
The sun's pillars bored me though, so I
    set foot on a small indigo place
below orange falls and hexagonal flowers.

I was able to stay there a fortnight,
restlessly roaming the buttered air
    inside tropical rock enclosures,
caves of foliage that canopied dankness.

Humming water and fetid air felt nice.
But the gentle leisure of itching, staring,
    distracted me. I frequented streets
in dreams, or in the paintings of dreams.

Large sidewalks of canvassed sunlight
concealed almost a city under that city
    while rivers waved in the distance:
the more you gazed, the more you saw

they didn't move. I plumbed down
and let that valve go and opened up
    a drain of some voice. I felt around
for honey, or whatever my memory of

honey was like. I scratched at things.
Not much scratched back. Everyday
   fantasy became my fantasy, so I
searched my steps in the mist of having

only this loopy world to attend to.
The doors, common and empty, took
   on within the avenues a mindless
smell of applause. I soon returned to

my crazy charting, often zigzagging
between azure doorways. Copulating
   clouds floated overhead. I rested
mine too. When it came time, I

knew you'd be expecting me though we've
never met and hardly a shadow goes by
   without reminding I'm your shadow.
In short, I've little to report. The coop-hatch

with its slant roof and missing bolt
misses you. Even so, our childhood sets
   haven't been drawn yet. How
could they be? You're still knee-deep

in a brewery, a concoction of mine that
proved you existed. Icecaps are melting
   they tell me. The sea's loosening its
girdle. The night has lost its prescription.

Newspapers blow up and down the streets.
I confess I knew you had better things
   to do. I didn't mind, nor thought
of myself as left behind, assuming fate

or chance had set us this way, fragments
on a map, drawn together, tilted apart,
   with only a body of water to connect us
to all those carated memories I imagined.

# AND THE CITY

Quatrains, peaches and rivers had once
been the clock of his invariable hours.
A swift green apron of someone's desire
and perishing fire. The city went on.

A crescent tugged at his stolid eye.
Veils of leaves laundered his step.
A thirst in lake-bright avenues meant
nothing. The trout moon dropped.

But now, after all this time and absence,
after the beautiful motors of dusk and night,
after the thrifty nakedness of sleep and day,
how could he account for simple water?

The scent was like a body left behind.
Memory some feeling nibbling his eyes.
Yet that was when he could be located.
And the city, a wealth of fire, went on.

# IT'LL DO

It was important to know such mistiness was elegant
just as it wasn't. The lagoon in the movie advert
suggested there would be a roan biz to take care
of these things, to fiddle with packaging, view
the obdurate dome out of which we stare
here, above the rest of the sad plain, in Dubai.
Here, above the rest of the sad plain, in Dubai,
we split into groups of twos and threes. Patrons
rushed the check; some gibbeted in the breeze.
It wasn't much of a day. Some consternation
was produced around the image of a lanky ear
others had seen in their balcony theaters but
that was a hoax, like a box of violets one looks
into only to discover the laminated texture
and manufactured trellis of a jonquil leaf.
Bernadette said Dubai this time of year was fine.
That waves buttressing the island bar would
be kind, in turn, and that even the salad bar
was nothing like the American version. Radios
quilted the night in a tourist's frank innuendo.
We didn't partake of that. Rather, I skirted in
shuttered galleries. Most had flowery breast
portraits, some were New-Agey photographs
of recent hikes in gasoline prices. One struck
my fancy—a child sunbathing in blue waters
numbly before some tsunami hit. The horizon
swelled, tossing like a restless sleeper's belt.

There's nothing much left of the town now.
Here, that is. A rabid jury's on TV hurrying
Easter banquets. Bouquets called May Flies
will be presented. Finally, we'll have jetted
back poolside, posing for such mindedness.
Preordained implications fall; the illusion of
a draft surrenders to brute facts. You know,
as one opens a pantry to find suddenly a pair
of panties. Then again, if we organized the roof
into different rows of suns, wouldn't the enigma
be the same—one of us leaving nothing permanent,
others scratching the gown-hem of citified trees?
Whatever it is, we take precaution. A pince-nez
dangles from the cubbyhole, spooled with tidings,
while we sit reading about more missing persons.

# DIARY OF A YOUNG VOID

Like any other, today comes with a fish in its mouth,
scales of German labor, vintage metallings, thimbles
skyscraper-sized, like the sprite's cherry body. What else,

in these typhooning sanctions, can be asked for? Granite
beds, droll breezes, even nostalgia mantling the foyer.

Crowded in a crowded world, you were my one steel O.

# THE WAR WE'RE FIGHTING NOW

There's this big war being fought now and it's being fought without you. I can't tell you who's fighting or what they fight for, but fight they do, lilac covering their foreheads. Their plan is plainsong, their uniforms a kind of lattice garb they put one leg through at a time, more delicate than bomb defusal, which brings me back to the topic of hoarfrost and the stories foretold about such people, the perverse difference between them. A town dreams itself along a river. Boys and girls play with a poundage of horse-meat. Grasses bend and quilt atop flowering ditch and soon a mountain arises until all belts are off. Old garters hang from linden trees. Fuzz spills from erect flowers.

We decided to daydream around what was left of the courtyard. The charred stumps were all in season. The light had the stoical quality of shingled brick. In each window you saw no one sleeping. No one scratching themselves, no one listening to the radio about a throng of paraskiers who wetted themselves along Cyan Lake. Down from the clustered ridge, some strolled out and observed the steel-pedal graves covered in nosegays and eelskin. Forget-me-nots from a recent skirmish lay atop moistened moss and emptied gas canisters. Little wooden men that cried real tears stuck out of the topsoil, musked with dew and dust and still-glistening shrapnel-bits probably come from that toppled embankment over yonder.

For what felt like years, we reminisced how people ever let their branches drift so far into one another's yards. Inside the split-level homes, ringtones still rung and memories of cod deliveries hung like fire in the quaint air. My father's people were a fisher people. They lived in a Tabasco-sized world. More dead persons are arriving back from the local fair now. Little can be told of what will become of them, though some have perfect tongues and that's nothing to sneeze at, having someone to share things with in the makeshift hayloft of a suspended carousel. Forget the stars. Nanny outfits and monster trucks preoccupy us. Other ideas, intangible as sapphire, like this abominable war soon to begin again.

# IN WOODS WE STUDIED

On St. Andrew's Night we grew into a castle; one of us
said: "This is the folly of lost rewards." Like a girl,
dapper, chivalrous, I knew the bat-hanging night
would be one more slipper left to post. Our hands
stuffed into remote pockets, those dental waters
oft-ringing, always with a sense of tamarind air.
You only add so much, hip to elbow, roundelays
to skirt, before the skittle-alley closes, Voyager.

*Feeling then gentle as I was arrogant, I slept in your clothes.*

# VOWELS AND CONTINENTS

Some peaches were gathered in your name,
    and that was enough beneath panels of
trick moonlight, parsing out phrases from
    clouds, asleep like a Subaru in the suburbs.

This time, we come as just one, indifferent
    to mealtime, caught with acrylic metallics
between sheets, waffling our waywardness,
    agreeing to save a cartoon milk carton.

In each, one of us sleeps despondent though
    eager to husk, brushing back delicious curls,
yet modest in the sloppy reticence of daily
    correspondence, rejigging dirty postcards.

I could see poppies doffing pinkish caps.
    I sensed in each bed a swart discipline,
a taste. Thoughts broken like islands, firm
    partners thick as the Kawaiisu and Khoi.

This life, in fact, is about rubbernecking space
    sacred as junk-bond litigants beyond all
purview, moist expectations festering our ears.
    So peers triumph. Yet in the jealous ruckus

of shucking, wincing, I'd still surround you if
   I could, replaying our loquacious pastimes:
breaching your neck's cover, its mint sugars,
   our awkward commotion iridescent once.

After it descended, it didn't cause much pain.
   Finally, your resale value was ascertained.
The meek leggings of fog, its crude smallnesses,
   follow someone walking a dog duly along.

# PHATTAFACIA STUPENDA

In panels of summer
we drive, coursing
and turning with
simple time, remembering
which notes to paw
over—the poor bird
of conversation, the good
chances we received.
Perhaps a proof
of La Fontaine. This
time out, I think of
seed raisins and
bottled gas, the bad
idea I had once
for six years, racking
my brains with
inadvertent letters,
fictitious persons.
I confess I got lost
here and there, as
New York is like
this sometimes,
thinking of imagery
of purpled cypress
as we leisure until
afternoon dawns.

Electricity. Simple
speech. These are
the sparse and rough
requirements: to stand
in the pebbled lot
with you watching
random things fall
into smile, considering
the advice of a humid
loom. All these matters
of radial color. Schemes
of highbrow living that
used to interest you.

# TOY HISTORY

All of our music inevitably is post-apocalyptic.
Leftovers sing the blues. Ocarinas hum showtunes.
Meanwhile, a serenade captions the distance:
a single figure stepping mute through rows.

The scene's eye is carried over rolling concrete;
such picnicked hymns and proud coral thunder.
Lettuce, arugula. And don't forget your disquiet.
Accept arcana, these stilling machinations now.

Can you read this? The slim noon, like an earring,
settles in confetti; the puce balustrade calms down.
We were here. This was our place. Roll call meek
and fleeing: a sanctioned raft, some psalm's plea.

# SOVIET PASTORAL

The big dumb tanks have all rolled away,
going over ravines and gangly voices of
remarkable underbrush that've told you
to postpone the art of the quattrocento.
I'm afraid what bears fruit remains silent,
is ignorant in these matters: elderberries
from Kiev, another sick uncle bowlegged
in the garden with exaggerated courtesy
all while there's pliable barley to strip;
stooping thicket under a barrel-mouthed
sky as blunt-nosed goats go trotting by
occasionally, the fellow yellow flowers
sweetly sermonized to. This morning
was another crystal envelope. Blinking
attention to visitors on the bare beach,
swollen mountainous views that could
throttle the sea almost. And memories
that snake around the patch of a thing
like music wafting in from the marshes.
In a ventilated computer shop, we carry
yesterday's orders, detour over to some
tourist's stolen ear. Channels, meanwhile,
run through the rain's rampart, transmit
a quite beseeching stare I recognize like
a Mongolian complex where kvetching
mothers squawk over key fundamentals.

A train sleeps badly. A fine drizzle sinks
into September's uncontested paunch.
That's really it. Often, passing the parlor,
remembering when the babushkas could
still knit daytime together, I'd feel a fire
at my back, like the sound of a cry being
radioed over fern-enclosed valleys. Dusky
couples. Peeling, lavender Metro hubs.
Yet here I am with you: in a broad quietish
boulevard, thinking what's become a game-
show of loving under ordinary circumstances
now that the engineers say architecture's
gone the way of the dilapidated chestnut
tree, if you can believe such things. Roses
become the past tense of someone else's
gross happiness. The Big Idea makes sense;
though now I know I'll find it hard. Vows,
reasons, joys, sorrows, even brick-lapis
on the lintel: there are too many affairs
waiting back on an unutterable shore. I
could just putz around, I think. Agitate
through love-borne supermarkets acutely,
stewing myself, finishing other people's
sentences without them or the next person
bothering to notice. I mean, why bother
these days when the translation of money
is crisp compared to morning's epithets.

*In his arms he'll take you,* a song croons.
But there are differences I feel, between
dozing and sleeping, like how a big valve
bursts when no one's looking, not even
you. Ongoing negotiations with the dead
are called for: a turf plot, hunkered down
in grass beside brassy, biceped turnstiles;
garbage mounds, wintry acorns, cliff-weeds
we'd rather not mention now nor ever again.
Streams crop across snow. Ruddy meadows
awake in the wrong season, roughhousing
today's lilac-shaded spots without shame.
I could paint you these, half-a-dozen other
almost Sicilian pictures. But there's no end
to the tender-footed satyr of commerce, his
Alpine politics, the Passion Plays that fester
in an arm-socket no bigger than a teacup.
This marble-gladed talk will reach its stop
soon, for just as it was naïveté that rarely
lay behind the works I've sold, less was it
a thirst for landscapes or people free from
the too-usual blemish. I was after the relief
of a new home to die in, to erect puckishly,
built beside old pavilions. Abject, foregone,
the molding somehow improves what little's
left of my bad memory, some manic sunroof
we squashed under. I remember once when

the solemn blossoms dropped, our bosses
called us to that strange conference room.
There were clever scatterings to name, mint
with starry lapels and adult videos we had to
arrange like rocks on the harbor's underside.
Truly, time does cling to things. Waves weave
stupidly to one side, routinely, repetitively,
but what the terrible news can't touch or
own exactly is this: I had trusted someone
busier than myself. Someone better than
perfection. Official bribes and folk balladry,
smacking of oily dungaree, struck through us
before we could even cross the next border.

# SOMETIME, EVEN LATER

I didn't always have this douchebag haircut.
Trestle of colonnades, the Arc of Avenues,
the terrible tremor mystery that accompanies
divorcée rhythm, sound and circumflexity—
if that wasn't enough, nothing would be
in these oafish hills, jettisoning for example
the dark harp corner of your self, slinking
across a tag-wall bestowed behind you as
cornered as could be, with a little digit
for pause/pain/pause/pain. You get the idea.

If my markings were a liberal-minded act
in this splooge of too-mobled monuments,
they'd first have to convene at a hospital-amphitheater,
unaware of plugged arm and chastened soup—
the [dematerialized] neuter and such; the thronging
but for black electrical dawdling.

                    "Languor,"
another mawkish pine, perorates with superb verb.

# SAMUEL TAYLOR COLERIDGE

I remember your hair's perm fondue
like blonde glass curling in the sun.
It had a northerly associative quality,
something quite remote to these parts.
We open to a stoop, as over the railing
a poinsettia meadow awaits you as if
you'd seen it before in the yard of your
youth. One, mind you, you've never had.
Nerve only gets you so far in a padlock
where bushes guard tempered watches,
spruce linen you wake to when no one
is there yet to really wake beside you—
idle and remote on cloud-mewing hills.
What dervish these late autumn days.

Partly tin, partly the huge arms of sleep,
I think of the hand of hands, the bland
studded caskets, the dew-brown regality
of one hour, its postmarked wilderness.
The mind, true, has its irritable spots,
absorbing much light but too little heat,
stony and diffident. It knows too much
some sorrow of chairs. Books open up
with snowy bronze Etruscan servicemen
gliding in and out of our daguerreotypes.
Meanwhile, your throat is a flower vase

no one senses; no stench now but dusk
and compass, which one winds stealthily,
coordinates changing, changed for good.

# ROCK

I'm somewhat unconvinced by the monumentality of it all—
the parable of horn and cornerstone when what was meant was merely rock—
stones and rock-piled troughs blasted by the lime of the wind.

Slabs like a granite sponge of sea-earth, a heaped shaping of whatever is
that cannot move. From the vantage of these mounds of sky and isles of blue
Aruban-bright, there are recondite, meekless, undisturbed sediments.

Tough, black rock. Uplifted hill of pebbled-chafed crags and chasms, decibels
of what really? Beautiful shore-waste. Barren-coasted balm. And beside
the beachside are ruins of something. Light assays. Grass is absent. Weed,

which would have to cut stone, is not here. Not in this pose, position of sun, balking air, other leagues of monotone. And on the bushless, leaveless rock—atop igneous agglomerations, sturdy and unsturdy stone—

is you. Young still. The sun tags your yellow shirt in the white blue. So you stand, as you stood.

You do not move.

# TWO WORLDS AT ONCE

If you're ready to piss off, then you could at least
explain why you won't be gallivanting along with me
this thwarted weekend. We worship at the same altar
of useless shit, and feel self-delightedly avuncular
when it comes to the showroom of wayward speaking.

Still, a testament thins itself over dubious, envious
strings. A chill swaddles up and down circumvented
blinds, and in this gasping late evening mess hall,
a particular contortion of how foreign bodies once
disposed themselves in minatory dress, eager for

close-ups, powdered in all the right and wrong places,
somehow says at least something about the procedure.
I've tried, all the same, during the wiles I've dealt with,
been dealt, in dragoon fashion, to serve up a modicum
of hearing what ringing noise is left behind each object

you had stood for, stood behind, or safely rummaged
through. More involved persons believe transmission
happens most often, ironically, in a culture like ours,
where items are not so much divorced and completed
entities, but are our insides' streaming fabrics, hung

up on a clothesline that stretches far into a distance
of inexact and perishable memories; that we've good
reason to behold one after another, second cousin,
as some chuffed ploy with nefarious pillbox alloys.
True, you've no reason to feel intimate with anyone

because you have no suspicion of ever again being
intimate with yourself. Baked goods of fair espousal,
the tiny matted surfaces of bleeding teeth, hamming
it up in front of no one in particular, grooming the air
for a svelteness no one could possibly bother to have.

I know, this all gets a little too tragic to be hot-boxed
properly. But no one said anything about you not
waking out a doorway into an entirely hokey snowy
scene, the plashing lashes of mechanical flakes adrift
over your two-piece bodice without slightest worry.

"Roger!" a voice could murmur in the eaves, retaliatory
for you never having dreamt up this quack scenario
before this too-late hour, when you're commissioned
elsewhere most certainly, at least the next life or two.
Gently a woman approaches you with a Black & Decker

power tool, some hurt token that proves which childhood
you were sobbing after last night, which gauche booklet
had to be held a bit too swiftly between perverts' thighs.
As is often the case, I'm sitting at a long table with myself,
several re-duplicated, steam-pressed versions of myself,

and the one holding out a mandrake, looking into a ladled
bowl, is probably the one who's addressing you right now.
Assertive, surgical tact could not be finer dressed than us.
Just as culture is a grab-bag spinning wheel, one to dart
along a cutting board, replete with sideways logic some

still love best. One version of the banal, spluttering day
we've been having is the typecast dialogue that's this.
Ambergris keepsakes and inlays that don't alter when
it is so much as make it seem trustworthy and defunct.
I'd like my identity to include, without preventing, you.

Even so, things feel a tad ghetto for me to go on like this.
Look carefully at where you are on the potted plains.
There are so many courses that could be unwritten easily.
Someone embarrassed as marble. Someone selling it.
The very thing we didn't like turns out to be everything.

# HO'OPONOPONO

The rushed flood wasn't much, but what is these days?
  Japanning myself in blankets, suffering the curse
and rust of my youth with shifts drying on the line,
  talcumed rain strops the rail, a bulgy view's outside.

I have perigees for your flare, O prom-thing one.
  After jouncing around, you should discover me
in this breech of peopled changes, like a gilt slit
  on bodily macadam where cockscombs spill.

The sun pronates to my left, akimbo—lowing at me
  angrily. It means quite as much as firm ground,
convincing you the dregs of my bed are sleeping—
  calling you in tune, appointing generals at large.

Orientalism aside, our hands are a coat of colors.
  When a shush joins us around the bend, we'll
prepare for a lift into the frontispiece tomorrow.
  Time to extort lopsidedness and old solutions.

Once, I wanted to be the greatest, like a boy
  in clogs, drifting through high timothy fields,
slumped in shade beneath a pricetag sexuality.
  Luckily, love stories are the same as others.

Now that that's over with, and now that that has
just begun, now that darkened windows speak a
little Latin, since the windows have nothing to say,
I amuse myself with dust that's also your honor.

# BOULEVARD RASPAIL

*I would tell you that I don't know.*

—GIORGIO DE CHIRICO

Today too is an impostor. The cut fruit,
The garbled scented meat, the poured egg,

The steamed milk, the fresh coal, lazy silks
Of corded rose—we've seen these before.

They appear then emerge quite naturally.
So, taking delight, one is taken by delight.

Drifting over corrugated space, wondering
Nerves become exposed, eroded and raw.

Fragrant lips of the minute sour closed.
Drops of peppermint drip onto wrists.

Anonymous weeping seeps into bone.
Shading windows, adrift over andirons,

Metal light dangles like a foreign lozenge.
Night cools, pools open, comes and goes.

My life has led to this. Searching in sleep,
Arriving at a corridor, not bankrupt, just alone.

# EXPERT COMEDY

Both in and out of the fray, articulating a sandbag
and theatrically exigent, riveting fashionable drinks,
you notice how others out there knock off a play
in mysterious passive voice, as if paralytic trees

had their own original progenitors to yell *Hush!*
There, a crow's mausoleum could be pawed over.
In this case, with your Bodleian head, its bravura
of evergreens and still crystalline coolant-dump,

you should notice more than silk-lawn clouds like
a man at the club window who feels *frisson* neatly.
To this we avow moral melodramas are reforming
what was left of us, ingenuous as tears, starched

by a broom closet called into real-life lifelessness.
Monikers and squirearchy mete the idiom for now.
So, like a blouse or bed-siding, you took comfort,
having to boil your shirt for mere peeping freaks.

Our new lives—transfigured, destroyed—vanish,
key participants in what's the central failure now.

# NIGERIAN SPAMMER

A boy in jockstrap is a joy forever.
He will be such, the puppet of a comb,
Handling strings and primal dramas
From *The American Songbook of 1810*—
Even stirring what your face bares,
Namely: silence, placidity, a mobility
Of so much rage and delirium that here
In the hapless flight of dinky stands,
Among someone's "true" deadpan gaze,
You could almost suppose the hooded
Body of your past life had reached up
From warm foam, gestured at you rudely,
Confusing "boat" for "bed," and begun
The inevitable.

I know this illness and wounded door
Reawakens many honest countries
As I speak to you, so that you turn
To the protagonist of your half-real
Daydream self and wonder, what comes
Next to convince of shifting materials,
The undiluted mercantilism of youth?
No one has that anymore. Our allegiance
Must be to busk about, quick with aprons,
Ample as a pieced-together version of
Sure reflections, the winning waters
Of a memoir, the competent attention

Of so many confident readers thumbing
Our lives with or without ironic salute,
Weighed through with false lodestar,
Given over to gay gangs and the tone
Of a single enemy, always a single one,
Some curly Pan a-strut in boxer-briefs.

It is the time of acute loneliness
In the plump grotto of a borrowed villa
Where you have to read out the anthology
Of someone else's mosaics, brittle posts,
*Cryptoportici* you'd never dig from caverns
In Taipei. Something incisive is trucking
About you. I can see it in your eyes. The
Beginning of your braids, several scenes
You would bring with me, have brought
Me already to, the greatest adages bred
From your possessions, in milky-stone
Memories miniature as breath, tasting of
Robust delicacy, the slim feathery organs
Of scrupulous birds epitomizing grief,
Complex backdrops that forge ahead.

We are all of us forging ahead through
The garden furiously alone. What awaits?
Pant suits, haunting brochure-snippets;

The National Museum of Vastness where
A single dung-covered head rises from
The portrait of a submerged moat panel.
Playful as Hermes, you ponder the first
Hydraulic pump, the thrill some of us
Get from stoking fudged brows aboard
Outmoded ships. Vessels of tomorrow:
They jumble in me now while my letter
Is still remote and not so efficient as that
System of water branching on the spiny
Landscape of the horizon. What I revere
Should have been revered by you. Instead,
Tender as I am tumescent, suburb outings
Happen, visits to the daily bread-basket
And the like. I am tightening my hem
For you. I follow down an emissarium.
Come, friend, zoomorphic as you are,
Kind to ruins, casually enclosed in space.
The first of many hostels awaits. Reliefs,
Curt transpositions of certain fine motifs.
Neither bomb shelters nor modern scarcity
Will impede this chalk-shafted peyote.
Let us strip. Let us curtsy in the buff.
I am desperate for my true love's dough.

# ADVERTISEMENTS FOR THE DISABLED

From here, we can open a segue and remind ourselves
of the turn we took back in the hiccupping passage,
an offshore road slick with fastfood skies, inbred rain
and other odd amenities that had bedazzled radio.

True, alongside these sober beach particulars you won't
exactly stumble into a gothic carving if that's your sport;
or be able to plummet into hives of ambassadorial bees.
Nervous rivers hanging in the hearty air have called us.

Naturally, we have a manual on our lap to throng about,
quilting this or that scene from another Chilean movie.
The narrator had told us about the sun-harvest virtues
as something had come into our thoughts as a bouquet,

disrupting elegiac niftiness, tilting toward summation.
Implacably so-so, those of us who aren't shocked will be.
And bowing without sponsor for copyrights of hair,
you'll explain to me such music. How it breaks the air.

# COLLECTION AGENCY

*1*

The pleasure of cratered statues. Flowers of fractured cubes and mannequin bouquets. Creams, Latin grammar manuals and the seams of torn fabrics. Yarn from childish dolls and little brittle hairs. An aisle lost in aisles of aisles alone. Rafters, ice-skating bandages and shattered ceiling candles. Taboo of wax grapes and petit-bourgeois artichoke convolutions. Panels of copper-piping virgins. Post-it notes and sprained-ankle pamphlets. The coverlet of your pillow. Unfathomed wheels and hearty transcriptions of Public Discourse. Pearl-eyed banisters and sandwiches wrought in iron. Letterpress monographs on widgets, inflated mistresses and elbow assembly lines.

2

The eyeliner of academics and party vials filled with real vampire tears. ChapStick. Names without human smell. Quartz balloons. A flea-museum automated with wind. Granite sponges and crimpled scarves. Busty mothers in plaster. Plummy coupons. Frigidaire neurasthenia, dispassionate conga-boosters and shredded winning tickets from future lotteries. Clicking of throat locks and clanking of cement weeds. Moorish minuets. Bibles and belt straps. Bootlace and garter hose. Bronze planks and papier-mâché debris. Doggy whistles. Ivory plants. Chopin's algebra. *Still Life with Bridle*. A Victrola sitting in a garden built up in straw. Barbed-wire lyricism.

3

The complete, remastered recordings of *The Labyrinths of the Sea*. Mock-up dwellings of Dordrecht and Arles and storyboard towns of Catholic philosophers. Afternoons. Islands. Carbon phonographs. Tawny tea-bells. Mobile phones the size of embryos. Continental breakfasts. Mesopotamian bumper stickers. Photograph of "Night" plowing "Chalky Rose." Film projectors and postcards (rashes of them). Vintage boxing clothes. Bookbindings of rather indifferent glue. One punctured tympanum beside miniature giraffe. Spigots and faucets. Yawning monitors. Banner reading: "There's still time. There's always time." Your image on the emblem of a gnome.

# ETERNAL FAREWELLS (I)

The moody set quieted down. The assembly
Reminded me of a token seen somewhere.

Anemones and anomies shared their gasp.
Someone lovely broke down signs. Spring's

On the tele; big daffodilies; ink reliquaries;
Printer plates readying for Summerfest soon.

Like a saint, I carried your presumptions
To see what was "run off" and what "me."

That object you had moved into the rear
Came priced: to watch a lover's long nap.

Yet I hate what impinges Easterful nuance,
Gamboling niceness or stemming our talk.

Placards were placed over the corpse-body.
A salutary banister defeated each porpoise.

Now what? A mule strains for pitted reach.
My mysterious speech has one gallery left.

Stewards no longer wizen on high-heels away
To Chelsea, Stockholm and storage supplies.

If cunning's my laughter, as it sees naked X,
How would I ever see you-yourself again?

In the range of the orange pony, a flower
Weighs more than the banality of names.

Daft helicopters wave to stations behind us.
Militant mums pound drums of their dreams.

God bless you. Tucked away, carted away,
And sitting by sprouts in goodly kind fate,

I have a prayer that weakens this treasuring,
Specked with the debris of your wonderment.

# THE HIGH PRIEST

If you could demonstrate something to me, anything,
of our late capital reality, 'twould at least be comforting.
It would assume operating prosthetics has a function,
that firmness and finesse are consecrated marrow too.

Or if, say, you could tell me more about the dummy—
its floral bodice and littoral sections, its waving airs
much like actual sculpted waves, of what things are
supposed to be once living, if anything's really living.

Either way, I grow tired in a rowing isthmus, fruited
with what abandonments the sky performs for itself.
I've suffered, too. Pierced as this diamonded droplet
held in front of you, set into the meat of your hands.

## MID-HARBOR

All such gestures may be inventions of nostalgia,
    ways of edging a tea-saucer future forward,
    poised perilously on a gilded table's brink.

We glance at ourselves with plaster cables strung
    over cheeks, snoozing the forest's alarm, turning
    to a charmed gouache with oblivious sentiment.

Asymmetrical styles wake up asserting their charm,
    a ridged wrist-flick of completion. So a man leaves
    a theater, dreams aloud his bowtie mate, fashioning

a virile something-or-another. It begins a rain droplet,
    a sedge: something full of oblong blisses, remote as
    dovetails, pitter-patters mute inside till we create

some sound like mice-feet brushing panels overhead—
    tiny destructions of mental logic—arcane dispatches
    of plumbing, some numb hoped-for apprenticeship,

which can be soothing. You get dizzy near the furnace.
    Stroll the museum. Object to a plant that's poppy.
    Soda, lima beans, crustacean provinces, oleander:

these menace and collude, while a billowy couple slims
    darkly, adjusting elbows, arguing incident & accident.
    I walk into a timely exhibit—an exhibit "On the Future";

its goof magentas have leashes with price tags. And you
pause, and stare at a corner that's not part of the show,
imagining a text to scroll out its full eye-deployment,

some journey committing you to take flight, go home,
redo woodwinds. There are no rewards until a shepherd,
wandering the park with saddlebag makeup, nods at you.

"I choose you," we wish to say in a terrain of love-making.
What happens instead to this blighted sugarcane? These
volumes and preoccupations—our old feline senescence—

like the agile way creatures paw preeningly when you know
the animating spirit's blunt and pleading. I can't pretend
it's my shift. I picture a saw, a musical abacus which will

notch and note out my life one day soon when I have one.
I'll retire to the country. Heirlooms of things that flaked
from me—interests, partners, tissues—will be amassed

in a jar, held in a darkness scrubbed clean from dewy grass.
Skyward, a zeppelin will set imaginary pivots. We'll outwear
ourselves, tossing off bodies in the manner Michelangelo

enjoyed it, surely. And at evening, when half-serious things idle,
grow meaningful, those of us who can massage mâché thighs
and partake of forthcoming cuts, edits, sartorial plans, will

be asked to a bake-a-thon. Tenable though truant, the sun
   won't mind. A rhyme of raisins laid out on your flowery
   skirt will do, or have to—the air almost a mid-harbor air.

# POEM FOR REVERDY

A brutal wind scatters
the violet. Nude #3
warns of the defense.
From a watermelon
pavilion, the rustic
crossing progresses,
happens, while gently
knells the day off into
an embankment of
neighbors. Strangers.

The zones of my
state are mineral. They
occur, dreaming a kite
met midway along
the headlong night—
taken in casual perusal
of stars, incidents, etc.,
which we can see here
from this postcard
humble and modish,
like emaciated granules
of pink rice. So this
is the way. Let's leave.
I have been meaning
to tell you the water
and well of this bland

silence, the grappling
of leaves tagged
to polyester suns.
A group of poured
jokes and oyster creams.

Familiar passersby
and garden voices on
the strong wind
of that repressed
moment. When
emotion drizzled
and quilted your
breath then someone
came out from bushes
of dusk to survey
the damage-strewn
bushels tinged with
copper moonlight
and a little grease.

# LADY'S MAGAZINE

As we live we die, adjusting the lens
    Of a micron microscope, listening less
        To ourselves than the brushing wind
            No bigger than an applet of wing.

The animal world slithers around us: tweets,
    Jerks, plots, and withal the brilliantine luster
        Of dense-twilled twilight enwraps us—
            Its equanimity no more archly costumed

Than a flag effect, a plain woven instrument
    For us to adjoin our attention to in russet
        And jute, pilloried for a silk-stitch second,
            Lounging across cafeteria aisles, versos

Of waterproof gestures in this phlox-bank
    Of light-patterns that articulate the instant
        A toweling sun sets at your caprine back.
            Yet if we loosen up for a final recreation

(Immured in "soft" glaze warp and colored
    Veniality, crepes of crinkled canorous phrases)
        Irises worsting your lapel's fabric will become
            As yesterday, convolutions of eternal hijinks.

Sputtering in this regard, you're perdurable—
   A flossy shiv of sea-holly you'd swear was some-
      One's hair while a woolly backdrop overtakes
         Our stumbling tumble, my dearest Coram.

# ETERNAL FAREWELLS (II)

Why do we enlist such innermost privacy?
The pivots of the sea are few and far between.

From cloudy bangs comes some recompense
And folly fluted with large margins of ease.

You were falsetto and harangued with mirth,
Bell-bottoms worn at the top of your skirt.

Gazing Cupid wore dastardly clothes in misting
Parks: salutations of breath and pestilence.

Blank as an abstraction is the abstraction I am.
Or the abstraction I would be if held like a light

In a glass of water up to light in a water of light.
I washed some of the beauty out that dumb day.

Your sobriquet sobered me up. Summer whistled
The laundry away, taking my number, arranging

Dyed shorts, taping my postcardlike friendships
Until a plow became weepily minuscule in bed.

Cloaks, clogs, lionish spittle of stock tenures—
All was yours, so I opened the rugs of my arms.

A city of mint julep crushed in my lavatory ear.
Combing your voice, I came back somewhat.

On an immolated canvas of indoor waterfalls
One must say how this changes and that stays,

Hearing on the lawn a pink flamingo's call.
Whatever gives green girth is gobbled away.

If you're happily flanked, then you're all set.
If you're tender-loined, then you sun the best.

Cowling at your iniquity, a vacuum-cleaner
(One of your sad titles) still scratches my jaw.

## AS OURSELVES

From here and there, I can take
Ownership once more over a simple run-on
  Sentence. Notice the farmer peons
And their ruby-tonsil'd hymns, like the one
  About the boy who drowned
And went on living his festive life without
  Even one soul knowing better.

  Gradually, the rest of us, living on,
Still live on. And some of us meanwhile
  Even thrive, if we can employ
Such wanton words for clinical realities.
  Thriving as we do, as we desire
By now, going on in such rocky areas,
  Getting a hold of ourselves as ourselves.

# MOUNTAIN STORY

You were living in a thimble situated by a coast
that didn't have a sea. You fixated on the idea of toast,
a purely epistemological pleasure. It felt riveting:
a bright spectacle of lashes left out on a ledge.

Soon invasive eyes of another commenting dimension
became the voice of your novel, the tear-sleeted sheet
of "feeling more," dealing less, the length of a décor
you could peer into for the shortest time, a passage

like a length of loose knots found soft to touch, almost
fitted, older than theater, being entire and brittle
as the "heroes of the possible." Chance had its
narration, the way our story continually evolves against

iterations—Germanic in origin, infecting, ruminatory
perhaps for a sweet morsel that's still dinted along
a bedpost sometimes sanctioned in the sleevelessness
that besets us best. What do you think of this postcard,

Emil? In an op-ed I penned sometime in the mid-80s,
I decreed I would never stanchion myself in either tether
true enough to feel elected to yet another altered ego,
the construction of a lauded poise, the thousand extras

that dillydallied with swaggering polity. Just then you
leaned from my dream-soup, describing "the detail"
as if it was your own conservative workweek: epicene,
agile, stupendously frowned upon but lifted up. Akin.

Hooplets, ceilings with oatmeal plushy frames. Orchid
tube socks with florid handlebars. *Lovely and sedentary*,
we said, though better to grimace, puerile as freedom
in the can-opened night with its barbaric embrace. Oh,

for we supposed our love will be as love—a scimitar.

# POEM FOR JOHN LOCKE

A sound mind in a sound body is a short
but full description of a happy state in this world.

I was wrong. Yet as people walk all the time
in the same spot, a path appears: our very own

Adam and Eve, for what worries you
masters you. Two players, two sides: one

light, one dark, and everything is nothing
but a dream. Reasoning and arguments are

of no use. Everyone pays the price. The stream
bitter, the fountains poisoned, our shoes gall

and pinch us, causing, yes, some stumble.
Trips the others don't want to talk about

because it scares them, but we all know it, we all
feel it—every day, every hour rushing by even

if there isn't time. They've attacked us, sabotaged
and abducted us, like a reverie where ideas float

in our mind without reflection or regard
of the understanding, whose survival is relative.

# THE DIALOGUE

The moon drops behind a stone field.
The dark listens.
Pearl is the cricket and banded street
where grass quickens.

A mild organ has started up;
dews thresh cribbed springs.
And I, I think of the mild times:
erased in department stores,
beside a blank figure, starving
under a painting of longshoremen.

Our words spoil the sprinkled weeds,
high and curling in the corded night.
Meanwhile, you slumber in the gibbous moon
or whatever's left of it, filibustering
among furled wings of lazy stars.

What was our job? Oh, right—
to clean the dreaming warehouse,
to arrest ambition, to score the aptitude
of others, figuring destiny out of women.
One lingers alone in the bottle-shaped alcove.
Another stacks arms and cauliflower crates.

                                        And still
timidity comes from months to twenty-four years
suddenly one day. Or so the adage goes.
As in a Carpathian tableau of sisters,
light shed within a storm: the message
is to embrace the blossoming obstacle.

So I wait here, examining merits, fiddling with a corsage
when not skulking nor noticing wrangled bicycles.
Like any talk, the mood must be around the message
to properly convey itself.

There is reserve for the sun now. Be still.
The thick wind will jerk free from the ward of our talk.
Look at what happens without much walking.
It's extraordinary. It *is* extraordinary.

# AT URUBUPUNGA FALLS

Puckish as we are, what really matters?
Creep through the room in a dirty gondola

with chimes under level-headed clouds:
that's enough, facetiousness aside. Yew can

grow off bark of Horn Forest, hum calla
rhythms therein, expound on procedures—

mid-vein, 8v7, etc. Myself, I am constantly
interested in Bekah studies, and feel fine

casting about, letting the immunoreactive
TV special continue. My parents are all about

plumb joints and that sort of trashiness
(which I've adapted to and gotten over).

I stare out the window at my penknife.
I press down on soft ions separating me

from my extenuations, my enfeeblements.
Limitary light preys on the ceiling. I snooze.

# TO A SHEPHERD

May you have rings of coral groves, and all the bread
    that proves man does not live on love alone.
May the starkness of inhuman instruments be yours,
    tempering a passageway through this ordinary
mountain range where the mountain-door dwells.
    In it opens all the new and old world problems.
Preferably, there'll be respite: civilization's slop—
    its grand mulberry; a withering spa by the sea.

May you know spritely pickled strings that throb
    like gentle adversaries underneath encroaching
sighs, with soft sweet splashes of blood-matter
    and ground-matter, smooth un-timbered song.
For always in my registering of life, someone else's,
    I come to a nestled ridge below a city-gridded
view, and dabble in thoughts that others poach
    unbeknownst to less literal things like who just

died. So a vague ceremony bobbles in my brain.
    May you have chocolates in muffled form.
May you feel ecstatic and hollow-eyed, for once,
    as you plead for a microstyle of fleet-footed
driving among hills; beeping a sheep-dispersing
    horn; checking every so often to see who's
written, who's marred or married, which season
    ululates its high-temple prayer all alone.

May the garrets and flower-slums contain ink
and silk to last a war or two. May brute force,
lacking its little stupidities, be like the little rain.
May your shirred head still be full with sleep.
Or, as the wind rips its furze-fuzz mane on rivers
and wagons a far way off, wrapping itself into
a golden ball, may you always have an elsewhere
to hurry to: wavelike, uncurfewed, passing.

# HAPPENTRANCE

I want you to pretend it's your turn to grab my ass
as a gorgeous swash of music rushes off the balcony
chucking its waterfalls of tin boules and tiny pins.

Now turn around. Admit it slowly, but countenanced.
The grand Unknowing has fallen down a filial street.
Salmon leap from your vacation-home lap. Call to it, love.

# LIKE SO

Who wants that end of the stick
Down here in a chaste lagoon?
Only a lonely bramble talks to me,
Intermittently speaking a name
Between Ovid and infomercial
Treatments. Lame and listless,
Before I can retrieve a small atlas
Of known perimeters, a theater girl
Hears me below where she wades
In the purulence set by a bugler's
Scale. What else is geometry for?
You won't stand this jacuzzi long,
Gestures blistered in the wind
Even when there's no wind, only
A piazza whose homely insinuations
No longer bolster our napping.

*

So you walk down a colonnade purchased erstwhile
    For a memory screenshot, raking your mind
    For what uncensored love we can restore—

Stamped bucklets and feel-good green thighs—
    These *don't-you-see* days. Tithed out of mind,
    Stumbling between strangers and marvelous

Indecencies that excite us, like discovering
A tender organ neither spirit nor body,
Some handle of flesh-puffed speech,

Odds spilling into time till we gawk at
Puzzling creases, embedded eyelashes
From Mumbai c/o Egypt, Scotland.

You amble idly, constituting all chivalry.
You spy ribbons that enwrap the porch,
Splitting crafty air like a notary's seam.

You bobble and perfume the common grass
After a leap, a slip, sweet blood rubbed
Off of a Quaker's temples: wasn't this

The dumb success you hankered after?

*

I will accost you like an idea caught in a fan.
From whence did it come? From the sky's
Bitchy monologue, crackling each knuckle.
Though I throb with born convolutions, my
Markings are sturdy as amber tooth enamel.

Stuck in a jet-hole and butt-naked for tonight,
  With a mastodon encyclopedia of solicitude
And modern necking paraphernalia—oil-belts,
  Noodlings, soft-stuff—I miss hearing about
Couples sharing tomorrow's genius apricots.

Their loose limbs' invisible scribble hushes
  Our daft ceremony, collapsing this business
Of lying about things, another's dromedary
  Longing, prolonging only others which gets
You nowhere—if you think about it like so.

*

I have a suspicion you dream up algebras to comb
Out the jargon of a body warming its soft foam.

Sometimes you crumple, a flower in the marsh,
Or stand atop the lintel stairway of bluing noon

Whose Magellan awkwardness has my number.
I multiply the same tale, often devising mermen

Their blunt general features, crass precocities,
One flipper of flannel to play in-house baseball,

Soothing blanket news to tunnel back to Austin,
The abstract fritter of stock exchanges, aggressive

Menus reduced for stiff gents to transparency.
I don't need a wand for big brawny statements.

My checkbook's crammed with nil germane info.
I lack proper antlers for leftover crosswording.

I need to bump-blitz. And judging from everyone's
Reaction, your frizzy hair out-gulled even the zoo.

\*

Here you are midcareer and needing set opportunity
    To see what policy-makers are made of, working
Both knowledge and a wedge-engine that turns but won't
    When you really want it to. Unfortunately, friend,
You have health issues to be traumatized by and cankles

To study under the bronzer-cream horizon: oarlocks,
    Rendezvous for one's country, research gains,
Depth-facilities whose skeins contain lofty oaths.
    You've bantered worry and hazarded "Big Talk,"
Knowing a word could carry not much itch o'er itself

Even in a dizzy diagram of waiting for a last oblique
    Companion. Fire grows. Ashy remembrances wait.
Shall we welcome them on a vulnerable giant skiff
    Forgoing garbage delicacies we cherish tonight?
Thyme hath recovered its lipstick and coverlet.

Cut it, I told myself, hobbling down the day's allée.
    There was no cove, just a twitching view of fevers.
Maybe you're exonerated from chariness, you know.
    But being such a "thing," like what I'm addressing,
Requires a protuberance no more real than a doll's.

What I want for us is this theater, to wear a sweater
    Together in the middle of barren summer leisure
And take no heed of that childish plot no one would.
    Walk me back now to the people-watching park
I love, and I'll offer you what I promised, sweet figs.

# IN LOCO PARENTIS

Why wouldn't your wife want you to bring home some books,
titles on the floods in Indonesia, or studies of migrant amnesia;
how flocks of imitators and legions of sorcery persist to this day,
until finally all that's called away cannot be called away any more
than one can take up their ladle of thought, and drive endlessly?

Still, the runes of our sleeping have brought us here, vigilant
as some piecemeal quiet of former life, inked and blotted
with an allotment of surnames and freckled appointments.
Trolling the registers, we trudge ashore. A sleepy lighthouse
rolls its lugubrious eye—the surf shot through with clouds
pure and loud as fissured light, a pyramid of constant foam.

# A WALTZ IN JEFFERSON PARK

*After this, what?*
*Singing to drying linen beside wrecked yards?*

We wandered down the avenue and waited
for the casual traffic to litter itself into our
conversation, as one does when alone in
the attic. This time it meant something else.

Later on, we quarried our sushi for the secret
that had brought us apart, like masons lost on
the deck of a shrimp boat with only a vague
cowlick of sun to matte our foreheads.

"It was like compassing the river for stars,"
said our tourist brochures in the exhibit.
But the sad joy of it was true. Exactly the case.
A bowl of cherries then rude expatriations.

Like the time I fantasized about your wife
in the Amphitheater of Nudes where supposedly
President McKinley sat, sipping his brown supper,
dreaming of some shorter route to work.

There should be some music for that situation.
This one, the one we're in now. Forever static
in the German grocery, staring into the empty lot,
waiting for electricity to squint and tap its foot.

# LOST COLONY

Laconic (but not lazy), this time the lights stay on.
The formal fields have their wanton way; cherubs
 go drooling in posterior exterior, dimpled afresh.
 Generously, music unzips, points square to path
token by no occasion; in need of jetties and sweeties
on some barren arm, a strap for each remembrance.

Gradually recipes and petite orders trade hands.
Waking ones prepared for in urban-most fashion
 come with speeches: momentary political unrest
 faced as it is fraught without irony or earnestness
 to keep it aside from lurid delicacy where waterfalls
continually re-brush themselves, perennially silent.

As so much can go wrong, a frontier of possibilities
 comes as resultant factor. Chances preen themselves
 on the abstract aftermath of carrying on: slowly
 the scene of one man in his own mental house
 opens onto juicy lawns, each memory perfidious
as the malodorous color green, sharp and stable.

In order for this to work, then, the scene one imagines
 morphs into a scene one already had: its misericord,
 the slightly novel, definitely designer-boutique of it,
 or the special way someone felt about an onion ring—
 devious architectures that assume no new raw stripe
until you can't go back, though covert looking's allowed.

Morality in excess of shoe stores and such penitent
    lecture circuits, oblong muscled people, their highrise
        indiscreet charities, redoubled fence preoccupations,
        garrulous fact-checking: in all of it though that was
what you were after. You wanted the thing real enough
to redeem pungent exercises of Victoriana: cream slacks

and the cherry lordship one could try to freeze in
    a tunnel with forensic goggles, those motley items
        significant because rumored derring-do passed
        over them. Little by little, breath had (or *hadn't*)
    shaped them. They encountered their room. Suddenly
you're face-down in perfunctory December. Content.

One with figurative hardship, sawtooth pay dates.
    Gambits are taken. Galleys are bound. Minister
        divas swap seats, not so much interchangeable
        as finalized: like a permutation's shirt sleeve.
    The rigor of sleeping reassumes its low position.
Infant tresses are bartered out of habits of thinking

and patterns not so routine overtake any old body
    in the missed journal entry of existing. Public
        furniture becomes our very own social worker
        doing overtime for affordable comforts: Teflon,
    engagement rings, vaguely spiked luncheon drinks.
If you look out on the world in its sizable wet chunks,

what had been boggling fairgrounds shows wrinkles:
    an orphanage becomes single-room occupancy,
        after being a hotel or some industrial hangout—
        the jive spot for motor tourists in a motorless city.
    Daffy light strings a certain body, one beautifully
at ease in its command of easy absent-headedness.

Gazillions of people evaporate onwards, as they like.
    To begrudge them that would be worse than not to.
        Only a few are thinking of the toolshed, the heavy
        way that formalized manners elect themselves
    in slushy openings, grafted onto this day, the next.
Your job: to murder each while no one is watching.

# THE ARGUMENT

The life we didn't live.
The time tepid as bronze.
The stacked air. The frozen rail.
The dripping of summer in drops.
The honey-trees, the brick façade,
the empty canyons of light through
Ferry Street and birch leaves
where a cloud drops a sock.

The sky. The records of clocks.
The wooden hours. The fort postcards.
The salvos of breakfast paper
on exhibit somewhere.

The gears inert. The girls inanimate.
The dolly. The one side of a house,
the other four stories high.
The weave of poor shoals.
The hoops of brittle violets.
The tubing of cubed lilacs.
The floorboards of the ocean.
The single step. The fourteen feet.

The rooms of little moss. The comb.
The apples. The cherries. The feathers.
The straw. The manure. The dirt.
The difficult gardens of your eyes.

The small fruits. The rubber necktie.
The sour voice. The nowhere special.
The lilting train. The crusty Queen.
The different kinds of musk at night.
The wind to tell us who we are.
The sloop of our look. The departing.
The trust. The funds. The desires.
The mistress. The bus. The sleep.

The day. The hour. The Highlands.
The liberal miles of marsh grass.
The leaves. The leave-taking.
The place. The sun.

The succession of rain. The rain.
The refrain. The whole song.
The meadow of the wind.
The meadow in the wind.
The passage. And yesterday,
the lying down to recover breath.
The argument. The raiment.
The tune.

The rust. The tribute of lost tribes.
The great minds of small force.
The tempest. The sleights. The self.
The valley covered in stars.

# SYRACUSE COURT CASE

Come away and meet some of the other winners
who are in fact quite eager to meet you though

this is quite the spraddled occasion, my thoughts
adrift like ivory placards of bulls against a sea,

sandwiched atop the open mouth of a clumsy
amphora. It's about as pretty as things get here

without much leniency. Each human personage
with unguents and genitals marks its divinity.

All manner of object takes on heavy breathing:
a certain ring on a black countertop not made

of silver; the usual skirmish of dust, arranged
for catastrophic snapshots; the looming fullness

of light, still fist-full and fresher than a million
heirloom flowers brought sopping from a field.

I read once in a honeyed tome the sexual myth
was distraction, a pretend violence we mend.

That distraction itself had a depraved-belly
repurposing, even if you feel towards it how

open windows in winter help the warm-wisher
sleep, enfolded in the algebra of dreaming.

Lately, after napping in the usual public places,
I've sanctioned my duller, growing skepticisms.

The trials of an aging eternal body, for example.
Isn't it like an arrow pointing the way, whether

the somnambulant rounds a clinician often takes,
humming his of her messiness in seesaw adjectives,

or like a real-life taste test, some home invasion
fondly demonstrating *yesterday's enchantments?*

Doubting is a sure means of denying life, the coarse
conundrum of musculature tied in one big knot.

Your hands like a pointillist river block names
from adjacent recall, the shapes so particularly

and distinctively null-and-voided, as if denuded
by all the scrum and favor we still have to have.

Like some chubby Damocles, you fantasize about
a type of homey awkwardness, slim and pyrrhic,

yet held outside of whatever "finality" brings you
finally, so that whatever this reduces us all to is

a/ bedfellows, b/ siblings, c/ English boarding
school attendants, d/ something gracefully else.

Maybe if you repeat things enough times in your
head to yourself without noticing, the old movie

will stay a movie, the new foreboding afternoon
will be regular in its movement, its buzz and lisp.

Because you've lived so long in secondary thrill
you've become your furniture, even though it

never becomes you. Rather, not *all* of you.
Another existential Tuesday sips its stew.

Following the garden path in a board game,
you wonder at how much longer it is before

the clippings derail and we're left along
a hilltop with rueful and squiffy speech

patterns that ache in tender arch then turn
to zilch. That I would alter nothing says

nothing about me. Does it say something
about you? Do you mind if I ask how you

got to this party? Your name rhymes with
Donner or Vincent, I believe. Don't tell me.

Someone's shrill snoring in the next room is
like a tail in the throat on a rather bright day.

# ONCE MORE, WITH FEELING

*HYDROPHOBE BORN UNDER WATER*

Forgive me for asking, but why in this mottled world would you expect another? Eccentric pilasters stand in the rain: *ruins for remaining ruined.* My dreams meanwhile occur in mercantile factory houses whose shelves represent gaps in the Now Culture. Reduced, though not so enervated today, the reality of dingy parlor casements helps me parachute to bed for lack of better thing to think or do. The lanky, still sun ravishes an arching colonnade.

When the sun fails off harbor and I'm still second-rate, arborisms notwithstanding, will you still love me? When noxious flax falls from the ledge and hedges wink back to their indubitable brink, will you still etc.? I trek nominal distances, districting perfumeries. My port rolls hard to ruddy, slapping waves. Tongue depressors are whatever's left of the city—its lisping fantasia of blue parades, airy sundries, exotic krill, mercenary hand-goods.

I come to cuddle thee. A scrapheap of odds and mostly ends. Guipure, Carrickmacross, Antwerp—lace swabs which pattern brides—are yours. Over the Circassian mountains, refugee winds do their thing, ensconced in mojo beyond translation. Cherkesskas, fairies, a bashlik float down the Psou without the slightest litmus test of failure to the contrary. I suffer gladly an arabesque. Field marshaling shows—unlike this country—you still exist.

I go into the houses of little angels and almost leave a good man.

Refer to whatever you want. Just make it local and habitually assuaged with sprockets, hanging or inserted in profound manner, like naked feet passing across skies. (It was a museum of accidents but also accents: Chicory, chromium, bone-yellow something.) Our seductive spills were brought out back near a hose, unbuckled, stripped, meant to bend over, describe English riding coats, thumb through tax slips, recite cardboard delicacies.

Please know from the crackpot of my canary affections, authority junkie that I am, my honeydew hairdo is not so much new as new to you. A pair of underwear restores you to its sense. Dreams autofluff off the bed like quizzical ladykins. You clasp dry racks. You snort a little tune to yourself, chthonic as ever. You lean into a grudge and out plops, intricately, a pidgin civilization: smoke without color, window without testament, needlessly attained.

# PLEASE EXCUSE OUR APPEARANCE . . .

Just as one surfaces upstream to see what one
had been consuming these many churlish,
gulag-y years, so too did I sweep myself up
in clammy quiet unplanned before hence.

At random, I investigate "timers," deterred vetoes,
plucking an orator's mug down from the shelf,
examining patchwork on the reverse side of a portrait,
hell-raising not seldom over the tire-farm outside.

Old films, and affectionate bugles that fettle
neatly in a concave dream, they were there, too.
All spit and rust in abiding hum. But I, I had
a new momentum to achieve. A turtled sense, call it.

Bleak striations that had mattered for little in
the great gray suburb—that one time or another,
everyone lives in—suddenly grew luminary, even
as luxury meant rugged oxygen, a conceit of time.

What do you think medicine is about? Is it
about finding a way along other people, those
more lost? Surgeon projectiles? Inexplicable love
of tentacled wetness? Modern gills & frills, etc.?

Whatever atmosphere you are going to live in now
it will be jerrybuilt by programmed discourses,
a diurnal trustiness that comes from splitting
the body, its sententious comb-over. Grave wax.

Yet I'm a person. And thanks to the court's wandering
sentence, I've bagatelles to dispatch, maids' alarums
to surfeit as much as famish. I dally. I seek proper
chevrons, though these environs are but tame junk.

# PROUD HAND

There are few cliffs here but the largesse of cold hours.
Lightness of breath maintains the western skies.
Winter, painters, this marble path . . .
What else calls to a carpet of bees, and burnt air?

Child of the wind-honored Yucatan, the sea's feet
are your unhappy exhibition. The prospecting pictures
grow, but gravity grows too, steep as blue
sea-salt, red as the gummed grass of wildflowers.

# THE LATE PARADE

*Rien ne me rend plus heureux que de sortir dans
la campagne et de peindre ce que je vois.*

—HENRI ROUSSEAU

Aglitter in the dromedary dawn
with cold rubles, the old cyclone
boasts come what come may, sir.
Like a silly curlicue, for instance,
that you called August. It too had
a way, prescient and plunderable,
a mix of corsage and assemblage,
or coconut if you can imagine it.

A wax cylinder in the wind was
carrying us chevalierly through
the alphabets of petite longings,
our gumption of restless itching.
If we stop here it's because here
it's thick dusk. Streaming ribbons
from the sun, yellow fields of sky
matriculating without thinking.

Slowly, the aperture goes bronze
squinting in the marble harbor,
guffawing, crocheting a speech.
The morning buildings are air

sugared with stiff upper lip.
Clipped romance butters our
pockets with comic-book accents,
pocked lingo and perfumed lint.


Yesterday, the dazzlement washed us
away like laundry boats bedraggled
    toward a ventilated hexagon of sea,
its coils and plungers, its plumber's tape
    amid lulling processions of joggers.


One spring patio is for rodeos
niggled with iodine figures, weaved
    tapestries inside vast *tuileries*.
But that reminds me, how exactly
    do words form brittle histories—


rummaging a basement heap, a guttural
section, suppose, or an anatomical plane,
    a slice of what should be and has been said
but wasn't, like some yogurty radio static
    giving way assuredly to sweet hosannas.

We bench-press archways with our eyes
recalling a time when we actually had eyes.
Yes, that was eons ago, gazing inside at TV
bunkers as Shock-&-Awe hunkered down

for supper, a roseate ghostly assembly line
producing but bruise. I could use a good one
come to think of it. And nickeled-and-dimed,
halter-top waters rise. Ferries a-glint with

restaurant dementias. Some happenstance
meant to be talked about. We'll have to let be,
with addled doo-wop and haughty pince-nez.
Alone here in the river walk you buoy it all.


You, walking stick, are emptier in a crowd,
though not as empty as one.
Amateur, I'm watching your surveys shrug
to the ground, dear and ruthless. The

fiesta has begun. And waffling in the breeze,
this is the time to reprogram
an ideogram or two, flinging pants off
for stoic sleepiness.

Dreams have the following architecture:
      metallic substance, pursuant laws
of mineralness. Vague plunder of booty,
      plastic robe of pearls. Sesame

pirates of our wonderfully dull childhood
      where a perverted man
usurps your surname and wanders the lawn,
      sprinkling reindeer tears.

Just as to love is to doze, so what I crave
      is to nose about. I, however,
in 17th-century fashion, stare at your chaps
      of frolicking gold, apparel

that includes a spigot, which cargoes some
      mumbling grudge in its hull
quarters to Tribeca. There we can arrange
      a spotted coordinate for the Star,

a strait pass that was kindred, mortal. Now
      resume the pose. Walk, rub, walk.

It only takes a brochure in your palms to let me see
    native Indias and corpulent Africas open gently
your cornet wrists, your marigold-clumped brow.

People should be able to account for something in
    what they desire or they roam fore'er, secluded
under western bandannas. This leads to reclusiveness.

Extreme passivity, pus ocher and the like. General
    spiels of uneasiness. I should know, happening to be
one myself, a curmudgeon crayfish like Fantômas.

A board was laid out. It had your legs on it, suspended
    scissor-like. A mode I knew from albums. Speaking
of which, one bum was overheard saying to the other,

"I like your bum." Quite moving mumbo-jumbo really.
    One door slices us to the next, the tunnels funnel us
into faraway space with pristine shops. You snicker to

friends across absolute distance. They always ask
    me the fable of my life, the accurate one, replete
with liquid bones to pick at or throw as testimony.

I prefer sassafras to crème brûlée on any given day.
    Brutal and cunning, but unknown, I love cyclists.
So a cloud curtailed me. And I awoke horizon.

The result
of such
expressiveness cannot
be denied.
Especially honey,
figures of
rain buttressing
cheeks with

small change—
contingencies due—
and this
mosaic: a
Giotto chapel
we'll name
our stone-braced
embodiment. Neither

reconditioning nor
resurrection needed
to become
The Possible.
You once
told me,
first giving
up. Give

up *what*?
A stripper
made in
toothy encaustic.
Boring. We
were literally
boring holes
in spy

stations. Calling
this all
a pipe-dream,
a.k.a. Yourself,
a something
for our
lips, sandwiched
in stares

stuck in
Porta-Johns. This
kind of
looking isn't
seeing. This
kind of
consumption 'tis
blindness. An

igloo rug—                    and near
it's not                      to us,
enough to                     picking up
be relative                   the phone
to example                    one day
and talk                      saying clearly
art for                       but only
the dear                                    "And?"


I take refuge in each skittery movement and moment
    I'm given when not forced to dwell on a monument.
Iron's the last bastion afforded to a materialist state.
    Next to gentle gardens, for a bit, we argued. Polluted

scales were a kind of resolution to wrestle us from
    ourselves, though I kept noticing the way our lips
pinched themselves accidentally, how vanity roped
    around our waist, delicate and burnt, as if dread

had come into the room with a waltz on our breath.
    At such gestured pace, you induce a sigh. Yes, you
ignorant child, those fireworks were yours . . . This time
    they were. Pyrotechnics fade. Experiments not

talked about until today in the skyrise of cabinets
and windows of papers flustered from sunlight
rise like a Goth girl costumed in hardened beeswax
whose tattoo reads *Buried on the Breath of Dawn.*


Wonder needed, patois needed, monkey brains optional.
Suitors needed, comforters needed, lactose-tolerance optional.
Spray-painted suits, undulating lanterns, scenes of frantic night
all for a checkbook that I would seize before surrendering

my love of the real. One who will be for the future, if only
to turn back his long and lioned head with remorse code.
Acknowledging acknowledgments. Like a magnet we drifted
in a boy's blink for years not knowing we were drifting.

It *is* always dusk here. Mechanical animals wait for us.
We wait for each other. Berry-eyed and bituminous, a tortoise
of waiting and wanting, mating and pray mantising. So
what are you really interested in, Pythagoras?

Things as they are, or judgments? Careful, the truth's a pill,
so chew before swallowing. Maybe it's just a *trompe l'œil*
effect, on second thought. Even so, it is what it is, and
what it is, we must swallow. And we do. We do.

# Notes

*Caravaggio in Naples*

This poem is for David McConnell and Darrell Crawford, in memory of their inspiring hospitality in Naples, Italy. "One cannot be sincere and seem so too" paraphrases André Gide. The phrase "the Virgin's blue marquee" is indebted to Sister Wendy's video lecture on Bellini available on YouTube; "always-already" to Jacques Derrida's *Work of Mourning* (edited by Pascale-Anne Brault and Michael Naas). Some words are also indebted to various texts within Pier Paolo Pasolini's *Stories from the City of God* (translated by Marina Harss).

*The Bride*

This poem incorporates phrases from Hart Crane's unpublished poetry manuscripts housed at Columbia University on microfilm.

*The Relay Station*

This poem is for John Ashbery.

*It'll Do*

This poem is for Bernadette Mayer.

*Diary of a Young Void*

This poem is indebted to Hieronymus Bosch and James Schuyler.

*In Woods We Studied*

This poem was inspired in part by Thomas Hardy's *Jude the Obscure*.

*Phattafacia Stupenda*

The title of this poem comes from Lewis Carroll.

*Toy History*

This poem, written on inauguration day, January 20th, 2009, is indebted to the metaphysical still-lifes of Giorgio de Chirico.

*Soviet Pastoral*

This poem is for Mzechabuki Czerniakov.

*Sometime, Even Later*

This poem is indebted to Louise Glück's poem "Tributaries."

*Rock*

This poem, based on a photograph of Christopher Catanese, is also in memory of him.

*Two Worlds at Once*

This poem, for Mark So, is indebted to the films of David Lynch.

*Hoʻoponopono*

The title refers to a word for the ancient Hawaiian practice of forgiveness and reconciliation where relationships were repaired through prayer and confession. Phrases in this poem are indebted to Cat Power's song "The Greatest."

*Nigerian Spammer*
This poem appropriates words from Robert Hughes's *Rome*.


*Collection Agency*
This poem, for Jamie DeAngelo, is indebted to Joseph Cornell.


*Eternal Farewells (I), Eternal Farewells (II)*
These poems are indebted to Giorgio de Chirico, especially to his painting of the same name.


*The High Priest*
This poem is for Zachary Pace.


*Mid-Harbor*
This poem, indebted to R. B. Kitaj's painting *Where Railroads Leave the Sea*, is for Mark Strand.


*Mountain Story*
This poem appropriates words and phrases from the essays of Susan Sontag.


*Poem for John Locke*
This poem appropriates the words of the English philosopher John Locke, as well as the character John Locke from the television drama *Lost*. It's dedicated to Sarah Whitmore.


*To a Shepherd*
This poem is indebted to W. H. Auden's sonnet sequence "In Time of War" and adapts a phrase from Christopher Marlowe's *Dido, Queen of Carthage* as well as a letter of Emily Dickinson's,

which begins "I hear robins a great way off," written to her cousins Louise and Frances Norcross, circa April 1873.

*Like So*
This poem is for Samantha Zighelboim.

*Lost Colony*
The title refers to an eponymous documentary about the Sukhum Primate Center in Abkhazia, referred to by locals as the Monkey Colony, which was founded in 1927. An Abkhazian travel website summarizes its history as follows:

> During the Soviet years, the Institute was a worldwide-known primatology center which conducted important research and cooperated with scientists from different countries. The Sukhum Monkey Colony consisted of about 5000 species who resided in vast sections and cages of the building. The scientists tested various vaccines and medicine on the primates, researched the growth of cancer cells, the influence of radiation on the organism and even trained the primates for space travel. They were also subjected to research of stress influence on the body, high blood pressure, myocardial infarction and leucosis. In the 1960s the Sukhum Monkey Colony was called the Experimentalists' Dream. Over 3000 serious scientific works were conducted here. (retrieved July 2012)

*The Argument*
This poem appropriates some words from *The Letters of Samuel Johnson* (Yale edition).

*Syracuse Court Case*
This poem is for my father.

*Once More, with Feeling*
The title of this suite of prose poems refers to a season 6 episode of *Buffy the Vampire Slayer* (the television drama) of the same name. *Narts Saga* is indebted to Mzechabuki Czerniakov for its various phrases and references to Abkhazian culture. *Rochambeau* refers to the SS *Rochambeau*, the boat that first carried Marcel Duchamp to the United States in 1917.

*Please Excuse Our Appearance . . .*
This poem is indebted to Henry James and was inspired in part by exhibits of medical oddities at the Münter Museum located in Philadelphia, Pennsylvania.

*Proud Hand*
This poem appropriates some of its words from *One Art: The Letters of Elizabeth Bishop.*

*The Late Parade*
This poem appropriates some of its words and images from John Yau's *The United States of Jasper Johns.* "Fantômas" refers to a French character of crime fiction whose cinematic adaptations inspired, among other painters, the cubist master Juan Gris. The poem is dedicated to Henri Rousseau, and inspired in part by the Stars of the Lid album *And Their Refinement of the Decline.*

# Acknowledgments

*I would like to thank* all my friends and colleagues who have supported me while writing this book, too numerous to thank by name. A lion's share of gratitude, always, to Joe Weil, Thomas Epstein and Paul Mariani, for their initial and enduring example; to Harold Bloom, Mark Strand, John Ashbery and David Kermani for their boisterous guidance and constancy. Personal thanks to Samantha Zighelboim, Sarah Whitmore, Ceilidh Orr, Liam Powell and Bob Weil for their encouragement and faith as well as Simone Kearney and her entire family, who have awed me by their generosity. Also, I want to extend my dearest gratitude for the unrivaled craftsmanship of Richard Howard, as well as the faultless counsel of Timothy Donnelly, in matters poetic as well as everything else. Finally, utmost supersonic thanks to my family: Terry, Peter and Matthew—for your love that continues all.

# About the Author

*Adam Fitzgerald* was born on Staten Island and raised in New Jersey. He attended Boston College and Columbia University and is founding editor of the poetry journal *Maggy*. He currently teaches creative writing and literature at Rutgers University and The New School. He lives in New York City.